GETTING TO KNOW
THE WORLD'S
GREATEST COMPOSERS

JOHANN SEBASTIAN

BACH

WRITTEN AND ILLUSTRATED BY MIKE VENEZIA

CONSULTANT
DONALD FREUND, PROFESSOR OF COMPOSITION, INDIANA UNIVERSITY SCHOOL OF MUSIC

CHILDREN'S PRESS®
A DIVISION OF GROLIER PUBLISHING
NEW YORK LONDON HONG KONG SYDNEY
DANBURY, CONNECTICUT

*A special thanks to the Music Department at Grace Lutheran Church
and School in River Forest, Illinois, especially Dr. Richard Hillert
and Mr. John Folkening.*

Photographs ©: AKG London: 3, 18, 20, 24, 25, 27, 30, 31; bildarchiv preussischer kulturbesitz: 9;
Corbis-Bettmann: 10, 14, 32; Erich Lessing/Art Resource, NY: 6 bottom; The Peirpont Morgan
Library, Mary Flagler Cary Music Collection/Art Resource, NY: 21; Scala/Art Resource, NY: 6 top, 8.

Visit Children's Press on the Internet at:
http://publishing.grolier.com

Library of Congress Cataloging–in–Publication Data

Venezia, Mike.
    Johann Sebastian Bach / written and illustrated by Mike Venezia.
        p. cm. — (Getting to know the world's greatest composers)
    ISBN 0-516-20760-1 (lib. bdg.)   0-516-26352-8 (pbk.)
    1. Bach, Johann Sebastian, 1685-1750—Juvenile literature.
  2. Composers—Germany—Biography—Juvenile literature.   I. Title.
  II. Series: Venezia, Mike.   Getting to know the world's greatest
composers.
  ML3930.B2V46   1998
  780' .92—dc21
  [B}   97-25756
                                                                CIP
                                                             AC MN

A portrait
of Johann
Sebastian
Bach as a
young man

Johann Sebastian Bach was born in the German town of Eisenach in 1685. During his lifetime, J. S. Bach was known more as a great harpsichord player and organist than as a composer. Most of the beautiful music he wrote didn't become popular until many years after he died.

Johann Sebastian Bach came from a large family of musicians. More than seventy of his uncles, cousins, brothers, and other relatives made their livings as musicians, choirmasters, and composers. There were so many musical Bachs in Germany that in some areas, being a

Bach meant the same thing as being a musician.

Every year, members of the Bach family got together for a reunion. They had a great time playing their favorite music and then making up funny songs that kept them laughing for hours.

Johann Sebastian Bach played and composed his music during a time known as the Baroque period. In the 1600s and 1700s, everything in Europe seemed to have a grand, fancy, and decorative feeling to it. Art and architecture were created to show off the palaces and homes of kings, queens, dukes, and wealthy businessmen.

A painting by Baroque artist Peter Paul Rubens (above) and a stairway inside a Baroque German palace (left)

Baroque music also had kind of a grand, decorative feeling. It was often filled with the sounds of voices, violins, trumpets, and flutes, each playing different melodies at the same time. J. S. Bach was an expert at making complicated Baroque pieces sound natural and pleasing.

Wealthy people would listen to their favorite Baroque music at royal court gatherings or at the opera. Regular everyday people could hear wonderful choral and organ music in their local churches.

Musicians playing during a European court gathering in the early 1700s

Johann Ambrosius Bach, the father of Johann Sebastian Bach

Town musicians often played at celebrations and special events. J. S. Bach's father was a town musician. He probably taught his son to play the violin and introduced him to other instruments.

When J. S. Bach (who was usually called Sebastian) was nine years old, a very sad thing happened—his mother died. Then, only a year later, his father died, too.

A sad Sebastian Bach went to live with his older brother, Christoph, in the nearby town of Ohrdruf. Christoph Bach was known as an excellent church organist. He not only taught Sebastian to play the harpsichord and organ, but how to tune and fix broken organs.

Organs being built and repaired in the early 1700s

Johann Sebastian Bach tested and repaired
organs in different towns around Germany.
It was one of the ways he made extra money
throughout his life.

When Sebastian was fifteen years old, he left his brother's home to look for a job. He traveled two hundred miles on foot to the town of Luneburg. There he attended school and became a member of the church choir.

This was the beginning of many trips Sebastian would take during his life. He was always looking for the best music job he could get. Sometimes, his music jobs came along with chores that weren't very pleasant. When he was seventeen years old, Sebastian got a great job as a violinist in the royal court at Celle, Germany. But as part of the job, he also had to remove slop from the kitchen every morning!

As he moved to different towns, working
as a choirmaster (a person who leads a choir),
musician, or church organist, J. S. Bach
learned more and more about music.

A 17th-century organist (left) and a photograph of one of the organs played by Bach (right)

Johann Sebastian Bach took side trips, too. He wanted to listen to well-known organists and composers to get ideas for his own music. On one trip, he heard a famous organist named Dietrich Buxtehude play. Sebastian was inspired by Buxtehude's animated and imaginative music. Soon Sebastian started creating new and exciting music in his own style.

One of Bach's most famous organ compositions during this time is called *Toccata and Fugue in D Minor*. This piece is filled with big, powerful sounds. It had an energy and force that had never been heard before. Many of J. S. Bach's mighty organ pieces have been known to cause church rafters and windows to shake!

Johann Sebastian Bach was a very religious person. He belonged to the Lutheran Church. One important type of musical piece he wrote for church services is called a cantata. A cantata features mainly voices. It usually has a lead singer and a choir accompanied by an orchestra. J.S. Bach wrote hundreds of cantatas. In each one you can feel his love for God. These beautiful works were a very important part of the Lutheran church service.

Bach's cantatas usually used hymn tunes, called chorales, that most people knew and loved.

In J. S. Bach's time, a church service could last for five hours or more! People depended on cantata music to keep them interested and awake.

Weimar as it looked during Bach's time

It wasn't long before J. S. Bach became
well known for his remarkable talent as
an organist and composer of church music.
This made it easier for him to find better jobs.
When Sebastian was working as an organist
in the town of Muhlhausen, Germany, he met
and fell in love with Maria Barbara Bach,
a distant cousin. Maria was happy to travel
around with her husband and raise their family.

In 1708, Sebastian got an excellent job in the court of Duke Wilhelm Ernst of Saxe-Weimar. Bach wrote some of his most important organ works there. Unfortunately, after a few years, Sebastian felt the duke was becoming too bossy. He decided to take a new job at a friendlier court. When the duke heard about Bach's decision, he became angry and had Johann Sebastian Bach thrown in jail for a whole month!

Being in jail was a very depressing experience for Johann Sebastian Bach. He couldn't wait to get out and start his new job with Prince Leopold of Cöthen, Germany. Sebastian and the prince got along really well. Sebastian composed mainly instrumental music for the prince. He also wrote the first book of *The Well-Tempered Clavier*, and *The Little Organ Book*. These keyboard works are still played by music students today.

After six happy years in Prince Leopold's court, things quickly changed for the worse. First, Sebastian's wife, Maria, died. Then the prince got married, and his new wife didn't care for music at all.

Prince Leopold of Cöthen

A page from an original handwritten piece of music by J.S. Bach

Soon, the prince started losing interest in music too. Sebastian felt it was time to move on and look for a new job again.

*B*efore he left Prince Leopold's court, J. S. Bach wrote a set of his most famous and popular works—the *Brandenburg Concertos*. A concerto is a musical piece in which one instrument, or a small group of instruments, stands out from the rest of the orchestra. It's a good way for an excellent musician to show off his or her talent. In the *Brandenburg Concertos*, trumpets, violins, oboes, flutes, harpsichords, or cellos play along with a larger orchestra to make up some of the best "feeling-happy" music ever.

If you are in a grouchy or sad mood, these concertos are almost guaranteed to make you feel better. The *Brandenburg Concertos* are filled with beautiful musical sounds that are sometimes relaxing and peaceful, and sometimes bursting with joy. You can almost imagine yourself being at a royal event in some duke or king's palace when you listen to these pieces.

In 1723, J. S. Bach accepted a job as
director of music in the historic city of Leipzig,
Germany. This was probably Sebastian's busiest
time. He was responsible for composing and
directing music for four churches, a school choir,
a university choir, and any music the city might
need for special events.

Sebastian had remarried in 1721. His new
wife's name was Anna Magdalena. Anna
Magdalena and Sebastian ended up having
thirteen children. With four children from
his first marriage, Sebastian was very busy
taking care of a large family.

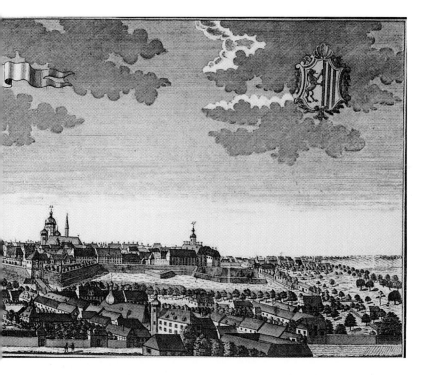

In 1723, Bach became Director of Church Music for the city of Leipzig, Germany.

Johann Sebastian Bach and his family

One of the many things Sebastian had to do every week was to write down and make copies of the music he had written for all the choir and orchestra members. This was a really boring job, but Anna Magdalena and their children would often help out. As busy as he was, J. S. Bach always found time for his large family.

Wilhelm Friedemann Bach

Johann Christian Bach

C. P. E. Bach

He was a loving father and made sure all his children got good grades, learned to play musical instruments, and helped out around the house. Four of Bach's sons became famous composers and musicians.

Johann Christoph Friedrich Bach

Johann Sebastian Bach spent twenty-nine years in Leipzig. He composed some of his greatest works there, including the *Goldberg Variations*. These keyboard pieces take you on an amazing sound trip. They start out peacefully, build to a swirling musical whirlwind, and drop you back off where things are nice and calm again.

Another piece from this time, the *St. Matthew Passion*, is filled with heavenly sounds and shows how Bach could put his deepest religious feelings into a work. And the joyful *Christmas Oratorio* has some of the biggest and cheeriest trumpet and horn sounds you'll ever hear!

Later in J. S. Bach's life, musical tastes began to change. People were growing tired of what they thought were big, complicated Baroque sounds. They wanted music that was simpler and lighter. Bach heard some of the latest music of the day in coffee houses around Leipzig, where college students and musicians traveling through town sometimes played popular new music.

The Thomaskirche, one of the four churches Bach directed music for in Leipzig

*E*ven though Johann Sebastian Bach knew things were changing musically, he decided to stick with his favorite Baroque style. Some people criticized him for being old-fashioned. In Leipzig, it seemed like Bach was always being given a hard time, especially from his bosses. J. S. Bach had dozens of bosses. Most of them had very little understanding of music.

Bach always had trouble getting raises or money for necessary music equipment. Members of the town council thought Sebastian wasn't working hard enough. The principal of the church school thought music was a waste of time for his students. And the head of the university thought Bach was directing the choir poorly!

A statue of Johann Sebastian Bach in front of the Thomaskirche in Leipzig

A portrait of Johann Sebastian Bach holding a piece of his own music

Johann Sebastian Bach always stood up for his rights, though. He often ignored silly complaints. When he died in 1750, he had composed some of the world's most beautiful music ever, whether his bosses liked it or not!

It's easy to hear Bach's great music. It's often played on the radio on classical music stations. There are hundreds of tapes and compact discs of his work, too. Also, many neighborhood churches put on free Bach concerts throughout the year.